First World War
and Army of Occupation
War Diary
France, Belgium and Germany

1 INDIAN CAVALRY DIVISION
Lucknow Cavalry Brigade
Royal Army Veterinary Corps
Mobile Veterinary Section
20 November 1914 - 31 December 1916

WO95/1175/5

The Naval & Military Press Ltd
www.nmarchive.com
Published in association with The National Archives

Published by

The Naval & Military Press Ltd

Unit 10 Ridgewood Industrial Park,

Uckfield, East Sussex,

TN22 5QE England

Tel: +44 (0) 1825 749494

www.naval-military-press.com

www.nmarchive.com

This diary has been reprinted in facsimile from the original. Any imperfections are inevitably reproduced and the quality may fall short of modern type and cartographic standards.

© **Crown Copyright**
Images reproduced by permission of The National Archives, London, England, 2015.

Contents

Document type	Place/Title	Date From	Date To
Heading	WO95/1175/5		
Heading	B.E.F. (Indian) 1 Cav. Div. Lucknow Bde Mobile Vet. Section 1914 Nov To 1916 Dec		
Heading	War Diary of Mobile Veterinary Section; Lucknow Cavalry Brigade. From 20th November 1914 28th February 1915		
War Diary	Orleans	20/11/1914	08/12/1914
War Diary	Berquette	09/12/1914	10/12/1914
War Diary	Auchel	11/12/1914	11/12/1914
War Diary	Lillers	15/12/1914	22/12/1914
War Diary	Berquette	25/12/1914	25/12/1914
War Diary	Norrent Fontes	25/12/1914	25/12/1914
War Diary	Heuchin	06/01/1915	11/01/1915
War Diary	Alive	20/01/1915	01/02/1915
War Diary	Heuchin	06/02/1915	28/02/1915
Heading	War Diary of Mobile Veterinary Section Lucknow Cavalry Brigade. From 1st March 1915 To 31st March 1915		
War Diary	Heuchin	01/03/1915	07/03/1915
War Diary	Aire	09/03/1915	09/03/1915
War Diary	Febvin	11/03/1915	11/03/1915
War Diary	Marles	12/03/1915	12/03/1915
War Diary	Auchel	13/03/1915	15/03/1915
War Diary	Febvin	16/03/1915	16/03/1915
War Diary	Ligney-Les-Aire	18/03/1915	18/03/1915
War Diary	Longhem	18/03/1915	31/03/1915
Heading	War Diary of Mobile Veterinary Section; Lucknow Cavalry Brigade. From 1st April 1915 To 30th April 1915		
War Diary	Longhem	01/04/1915	14/04/1915
War Diary	Flechin	15/04/1915	15/04/1915
War Diary	Longhem	15/04/1915	18/04/1915
War Diary	Aire	19/04/1915	19/04/1915
War Diary	Longhem	20/04/1915	21/04/1915
War Diary	Aire	22/04/1915	22/04/1915
War Diary	Longhem	23/04/1915	24/04/1915
War Diary	Simarie Cappell	25/04/1915	28/04/1915
War Diary	St Jan Lez Bizet	29/04/1915	30/04/1915
Heading	War Diary of Mobile Veterinary Section Lucknow Cavalry Brigade. From 1st May 1915 To 31st May 1915		
War Diary	Caestre	01/05/1915	03/05/1915
War Diary	S Sylvestre	04/05/1915	09/05/1915
War Diary	Neufpre	09/05/1915	26/05/1915
War Diary	Longue Croix	27/05/1915	27/05/1915
War Diary	Erkelsbrugge	28/05/1915	31/05/1915
Heading	War Diary of Mobile Veterinary Section, Lucknow Cavalry Brigade. From 1st June 1915 To 31st July 1915		
War Diary	Ketsbrugge	01/06/1915	15/06/1915
War Diary	Mametz	16/06/1915	31/07/1915

Heading	War Diary of Mobile Veterinary Section, Lucknow Cavalry Brigade From 1st August 1915 To 31st October 1915		
War Diary	Aire	02/08/1915	02/08/1915
War Diary	Berteaucourt	05/08/1915	02/09/1915
War Diary	St. Gratien	03/09/1915	12/09/1915
War Diary	St. Leger	13/09/1915	22/09/1915
War Diary	Monte Plasir	23/09/1915	30/09/1915
War Diary	Monts Plasir	31/09/1915	22/10/1915
War Diary	Cavillon	25/10/1915	25/10/1915
War Diary	Hangest	29/10/1915	31/10/1915
Heading	War Diary of Mobile Veterinary Section Lucknow Cavalry Brigade From 1st November 1915 To 31st December 1915		
War Diary	Hangest	01/11/1915	05/11/1915
War Diary	Le Quesnot	05/11/1915	18/11/1915
War Diary	Le Catelet	20/11/1915	15/12/1915
War Diary	Frirevlles	16/12/1915	30/12/1915
Heading	War Diary of Mobile Veterinary Section Lucknow Cavalry Brigade From 1st January 1916 To 31st January 1916		
War Diary	Frirevlles	01/01/1916	31/01/1916
Heading	War Diary of Mobile Veterinary Section, Lucknow Cavalry Brigade From 1st February 1916 To 29th February 1916		
War Diary	Frirevlles	01/02/1916	29/02/1916
Heading	War Diary of Mobile Veterinary Section, Lucknow Cavalry Brigade. From 1st March 1916 To 31st March 1916		
War Diary	Frirevlles	01/03/1916	26/03/1916
War Diary	Cumonville	30/03/1916	30/03/1916
Heading	War Diary of Mobile Veterinary Section, Lucknow Cavalry Brigade From 1st April 1916 To 30th April 1916		
War Diary	Cumonville	01/04/1916	30/04/1916
Heading	War Diary of Mobile Veterinary Section, Lucknow Cavalry Brigade From 1st May 1916 To 31st May 1916		
War Diary	Cumonville	01/05/1916	01/05/1916
War Diary	St. Riquer	03/05/1916	07/05/1916
War Diary	Cumonville	09/05/1916	10/05/1916
War Diary	Honval	12/05/1916	30/05/1916
Heading	War Diary of Mobile Veterinary Section Lucknow Cavalry Brigade From 1st June 1916 To 30th June 1916		
War Diary	Honval	01/06/1916	30/06/1916
War Diary	Grouches	30/06/1916	30/06/1916
Heading	War Diary of Mobile Veterinary Section Lucknow Cavalry Brigade From 1st July 1916 To 31st July 1916		
Heading	War Diary of Lucknow Cavalry Mobile Vet. Section From 1st July 1916 To 31st July 1916		
War Diary	Grouches	01/07/1916	02/07/1916
War Diary	Frohen Le Grand	04/07/1916	19/07/1916
War Diary	Villers Brulin	22/07/1916	22/07/1916
War Diary	Bethencourt	23/07/1916	31/07/1916
Heading	War Diary of Mobile Veterinary Section Lucknow Cavalry Brigade From 1st August 1916 To 31st August 1916		

War Diary	Bethencourt	01/08/1916	09/08/1916
War Diary	Hurtbise Fm	10/08/1916	29/08/1916
Heading	War Diary of Mobile Veterinary Section, Lucknow Cavalry Brigade. From 1st September 1916 To 30th September 1916		
War Diary	Couturelle	01/09/1916	03/09/1916
War Diary	Occoches	04/09/1916	04/09/1916
War Diary	Brailly-Cornehotte	05/09/1916	11/09/1916
War Diary	Frohen-Le-Grand	12/09/1916	13/09/1916
War Diary	Allonville Camp	14/09/1916	16/09/1916
War Diary	Morlancourt Camp	19/09/1916	26/09/1916
War Diary	Mametz	27/09/1916	27/09/1916
War Diary	Bussy-Les-Daours	28/09/1916	28/09/1916
War Diary	Hangest-Sur-Somme	29/09/1916	29/09/1916
War Diary	Montfliers	30/09/1916	30/09/1916
Heading	War Diary of Mobile Veterinary Section Lucknow Cavalry Brigade From 1st October 1916 To 30th November 1916		
War Diary	Crecy	01/10/1916	31/10/1916
War Diary	War Diary of Lucknow Bde M. V. S. 4th C A V. Nov. 1st To 30th 1916		
War Diary	Crecy	01/11/1916	02/11/1916
War Diary	Hymmeville	03/11/1916	30/11/1916
Heading	War Diary of Mobile Veterinary Section, Lucknow Cavalry Brigade From 1st December 1916 To 31st December 1916		
Heading	War Diary of Mobile Veterinary Section. For the Month of December 1916		
War Diary	Moyenneville	01/12/1916	14/12/1916
War Diary	Chaussoy	17/12/1916	31/12/1916

Army Form C. 2118.

WAR DIARY
or
INTELLIGENCE SUMMARY.

(Erase heading not required.)

Instructions regarding War Diaries and Intelligence Summaries are contained in F. S. Regs., Part II, and the Staff Manual respectively. Title pages will be prepared in manuscript.

Hour, Date, Place.	Summary of Events and Information.	Remarks and references to Appendices.
28/2/15 Hauchin	Larres Vara Khan of the Section, reported sick.	

R.A. Gooderidge
Capt. A.V.C.
O.C. Mobile Veterinary Section
Lucknow Cavalry Brigade

WAR DIARY

OF

Mobile Veterinary Section Lucknow Cavalry Brigade.

From 1st March 1915 To 31st March 1915

Army Form C. 2118.

WAR DIARY
of Mobile Veterinary Section Lucknow Cavalry Brigade
INTELLIGENCE SUMMARY.

(Erase heading not required.)

Instructions regarding War Diaries and Intelligence Summaries are contained in F. S. Regs., Part II, and the Staff Manual respectively. Title pages will be prepared in manuscript.

ADJUTANT GENERAL INDIA
-5 APR 1915
BASE OFFICE

Hour, Date, Place.		Summary of Events and Information.	Remarks and references to Appendices.
March 1st & 2nd	HEUCHIN	Ordinary routine work	
10 a.m. 3rd	"	DADVS Lucknow Div.S. inspected the brigade	
4th, 5th, 6th	"	Ordinary routine work	
7pm 7th	"	Moved Section with Brigade to Febvin	
6.30 a.m. 9th	AIRE	Despatched 8 sick horses to Neuf Chatel	
6.3 a.m. 11th	Febvin	Marched to Marles Attacked in open for the night	
1.30 p.m. 12th	MARLES	Marched to AUCHEL	
13th	AUCHEL	Admitted 7 sick horses - Section. Despatched 22 horses to Neuf Chatel	
10 p.m. 15th	AUCHEL	Marched to FEBVIN	
3.30 p.m. 16-16th	FEBVIN	Headquarters including Veterinary Section moved to LIGNEY. Admitted 3 sick horses	
18th	LIGNEY-LES-AIRE LONGHEM	Brigade marched to LONGHEM from LIGNEY-LES-AIRE Admitted 7 sick horses. Left one horse behind at LIGNEY but brought him over at night	
8-15 a.m. 18-25th	LONGHEM	Routine work. Received information that British personnel of Section should be armed with accoutrements Bands Rifles	

Army Form C. 2118.

WAR DIARY
or
INTELLIGENCE SUMMARY

(Erase heading not required.)

Hour, Date, Place.	Summary of Events and Information.	Remarks and references to Appendices.
26th LONGHEM	Received 5 horses from 1st K.D.Gs. + 2 from 36th Jacob's Horse.	
27th "	3 horses from 29th Lancers. Discharged 6 horses.	
28th "	Routine work	
11 am. 29th "	DDVS. I.c.c. inspected Section.	
30th "	Evacuated 6 sick + 2 cast horses from AIRE.	
31st "	Received 2 sick + discharged 3 sick horses.	

L.A. Gooderidge
Capt. AVC.

Journal No. 178.

12/5584

WO
5/5

WAR DIARY
OF
Mobile Veterinary Section, Lucknow Cavalry Brigade.

From 1st April 1915 To 30th April 1915

Army Form C. 2118.

WAR DIARY
or
INTELLIGENCE SUMMARY.

(Erase heading not required.)

Instructions regarding War Diaries and Intelligence Summaries are contained in F. S. Regs., Part II, and the Staff Manual respectively. Title pages will be prepared in manuscript.

Hour, Date, Place.	Summary of Events and Information.	Remarks and references to Appendices.
April 1st 1915. LONGUENESSE. 11:30 a.m.	Received 13 remounts & a horse (27 Light Cavalry).	
2nd "	Remounts since March 2nd inspected by G.O.C. I.C.C.	
3rd "	Transferred farrier Jones to 29th Lancers.	
"	Admitted 1 sick horse.	
4th "	Admitted 7 sick.	
5th "	Discharged 8 sick.	
6th "	Section transport and horse marsh under orders of O.C. A.S.C. 1st I.C. Division.	
"	Evacuated 8 horses from AIRE.	
7th "	G.O.C. Lucknow Brigade inspected section horses.	
"	Transferred 8 to 1st K.D.G.'s. Discharged 1 horse duty.	
8th "	Admitted 3 sick horses. General Routine work.	
9th to 12th "	General Routine work.	
13th "	Evacuated stores from AIRE.	
14th "	Admitted 3 sick horses.	

Serial No. 178

12/6502

WAR DIARY
OF

Mobile Veterinary Section, Lucknow Cavalry Brigade.

FROM 1st June 1915 TO 31st July 1915

WAR DIARY
INTELLIGENCE SUMMARY
(Erase heading not required.)

Hour, Date, Place.	Summary of Events and Information.	Remarks and references to Appendices.
1-6-15 E. Katsbrugge.	February routine work.	
15-6-15 "	Marched section with B. Echelon to MAMETZ.	
16.6.15 MAMETZ.	Received orders from Corps that all horses admitted to Section, if cured would be re-issued through Remount Officer & immediately struck off the strength of the unit when admitted by me. Took on Veterinary charge of 29th Lancers.	
16.6.15 6.30=6.15 "	Routine work.	

A A Goodenough
Capt. AVC

Oc. Mobile Vety Section
Lucknow Cavalry Bde.

Army Form C. 2118.

WAR DIARY

or

INTELLIGENCE SUMMARY.

(Erase heading not required.)

Instructions regarding War Diaries and Intelligence Summaries are contained in F. S. Regs., Part II, and the Staff Manual respectively. Title pages will be prepared in manuscript.

Hour, Date, Place.	Summary of Events and Information.	Remarks and references to Appendices.
1=7=15 MAMETZ	Ordinary routine work.	
22=7=15 "	Took over charge of Rattend Detachment at AIRE.	
9.30 am 24.7.15 "	Inspection of Section Transport with the Brigade by Govr. Lucknow Cavalry Bde.	
9.45 am 26.7.15 "	Inspection of Transport by Govr. Indian Cavalry Corps. also a Route March.	
31=7=15 "	Brought all horses from Rattend Detachment at AIRE (27 in number) into my Section.	

Ro. Goodercall
Capt A.V.C.

O.C. M/Orie Vety Section.
Lucknow Cavalry Bde.

Serial No. 178.

7750/CI

Confidential

War Diary

of

Mobile Veterinary Section, Lucknow Cavalry Brigade

FROM 1st August 1915 **TO** 31st October ~~August~~ 1915

Army Form C. 2118.

CR/388
3/12/15

WAR DIARY
or
INTELLIGENCE SUMMARY.
(Erase heading not required.)

Instructions regarding War Diaries and Intelligence Summaries are contained in F. S. Regs., Part II, and the Staff Manual respectively. Title pages will be prepared in manuscript.

Hour, Date, Place.	Summary of Events and Information.	Remarks and references to Appendices.
1.8.15 AIRE	Marched with Brigade from Aire to BERTEAUCOURT + took over billets there.	
5.8.15 BERTEAUCOURT	Took over Command of the Mobile Veterinary Section from Capt Goodridge A.V.C.	
8.8.15 BERTEAUCOURT	Evacuated seventeen horses from Railhead Longpre to No 5 Veterinary Hospital Abbeville.	
16.8.15 BERTEAUCOURT	Evacuated eleven horses from Railhead Longpre to No 5 Veterinary Hospital, Abbeville.	
20.8.15 BERTEAUCOURT	Ordinary Routine Work.	
31.8.15 BERTEAUCOURT	Evacuated five horses from railhead Longpre to No 5 Veterinary Hospital, Abbeville. Received orders from A.D.V.S. that no horses are to be received into the Mobile Section except for evacuation	
31.8.15		

W. E. Murphy
Lieutenant
O.C. M.V.S
Lucknow Cavalry Bde

Army Form C. 2118.

WAR DIARY
or
INTELLIGENCE SUMMARY.

(Erase heading not required.)

Instructions regarding War Diaries and Intelligence Summaries are contained in F.S. Regs., Part II, and the Staff Manual respectively. Title pages will be prepared in manuscript.

Hour, Date, Place.	Summary of Events and Information.	Remarks and references to Appendices.
1.9.15 BERTEAUCOURT	Ordinary Routine Work.	
3.15 P.M. 2.9.15 " "	Under orders of Quatermaster Gen. Ride the Mobile Vety. Section left BERTEAUCOURT & marched with B. Echelon to ST GRATIEN, arriving 9. P.M.	
3.9.15 ST. GRATIEN	moved into new billets.	
4.9.15 " "	Ordinary Routine Work	
10.9.15 " "	Evacuated 17 sick horses from railhead thereabout – to no 5 Veterinary Hospital, Abbeville.	
10. am 11.9.15 " "	Mobile Veterinary Section ordered to move to ST. LEGER on 12th inst.	
4 P.M. 11.9.15 " "	A.D.V.S. orders m.V.S to march with led horse party returning from trenches	
3.30 P.M. 12.9.15 " "	To enable M.V.S to return with led horse party a party in charge of N.C.O sent on in advance with another sick horses unable to travel quickly – These horses belonged to different units of the Division	

WO 95/11751 5/5/5

B.E.F.
1 Cav. Div. (Indian)

Lucknow Bde.

Mobile Vet. Section

1914 Nov to 1916 Dec

Serial No. 178.

WAR DIARY

Mobile Veterinary Section; Lucknow Cavalry Brigade.

From 20th November 1914 to 28th February 1915

Army Form C. 2118.

WAR DIARY
or
INTELLIGENCE SUMMARY.

(Erase heading not required.)

Instructions regarding War Diaries and Intelligence Summaries are contained in F.S. Regs., Part II, and the Staff Manual respectively. Title pages will be prepared in manuscript.

ADJUTANT GENERAL INDIA
−7 MAR 1915
BASE OFFICE

Hour, Date, Place.	Summary of Events and Information.	Remarks and references to Appendices.
20/11/14 Cairo	Took over personnel of Mobile Veterinary Section from 29th Lancers & 3rd Jacob's Horse, consisting of 1 R. Driffgadar, 1 R. Driffgadar (Saluti) 29th Lancers, 5 Sowars, 6 Sowars 36 jacobs Horse. Equipping section with Ordnance & Veterinary Equipment	
12.15p 8/12/14 Cairo	Marched from Camp la Force to Le Rock Station Entrained for Beguette.	
6.30p 9/12/14 Beguette	Arrived Beguette. Billeted for the night.	
10.30am 10/12/14 Beguette	Marched to Auchel. Billeted for the night.	
11 am 11/12/14 Auchel	Marched to Lillers & Billeted section.	
3.30pm 15/12/14 Lillers.	Entrained 11 sick horses to Mediginal Hospital.	
4pm 20/12/14 Lillers.	Entrained 25 sick horses to Abbeville Hospital.	
4pm 1/1/15 Lillers.	Entrained 11 sick horses & 1 mule to Mediginal Hospital	
7.30am 22/1/15 Lillers	Marched Section to Mount Sainte Eloi.	
1pm 25/1/15 Beguette	Entrained 3 sick horses for Mediginal Hospital	
11 am 25/1/15 Mount St. Eloi. Veterinary Section marched to Aubelin with the R. Driffgadar. Mobile Veterinary Section in village of Bergenene.		

Army Form C. 2118.

WAR DIARY
or
INTELLIGENCE SUMMARY.
(Erase heading not required.)

Instructions regarding War Diaries and Intelligence Summaries are contained in F.S. Regs., Part II, and the Staff Manual respectively. Title pages will be prepared in manuscript.

Hour, Date, Place.	Summary of Events and Information.	Remarks and references to Appendices.
4.30 p.m. 6/1/15 Heuchin	I reported my departure to G.O.C. Brigade, for 5 days leave in England. Section handed over to Farrier Hogg A.V.C.	
11.30 a.m. 11/1/15 Heuchin	Arrived back from 5 days leave.	
12.30 p.m. 20/1/15 Airie	Entrained 29 sick horses for Veterinary Hospital Neufchatel.	
2.30 p.m. 1/2/15 Airie	Entrained 19 horses to Veterinary Hospital Neufchatel.	
6/2/15 Heuchin	Received 1 horse from 36th Jacob's Horse to replace a casualty in the Section.	
8/2/15 Heuchin	Received 1 horse from 29th Lancers. This sick horse is auctioned by A.D.V.S. 1st Indian Cavalry Division since the extra cart given to the section.	
8/2/15 Heuchin	Reported to A.D.V.S. 1st Indian Cavalry Division re my Farrier, YARA KHAN 38th Jacob's Horse, as to his treatises at his work.	
10 a.m. 17/2/15 Heuchin	Section inspected by G.O.C. Lucknow Cavalry Brigade.	
19/2/15 Heuchin	Returned 6 mules + one sword to the 29th Lancers + one sword to the 38th Jacob's Horse, by order of G.O.C. Brigade	

WAR DIARY Mobile Veterinary Section, Lucknow Cavalry Brigade
Army Form O. 2118.

INTELLIGENCE SUMMARY.

Hour, Date, Place.	Summary of Events and Information.	Remarks and references to Appendices.
10.a.m. 15 April 1915 FLECHIN	Proceeded in Court Martial on No 1091 Pte Green AVC of my section.	
" " 16th–17th LONGHEM	Admitted 4 sick horses. General Routine Work.	
" 18th "	Promulgated sentence of Court Martial on No 1091 Pte Green AVC	
" 19th AIRE.	Evacuated 18 horses to NEUF-CHATEL.	
" 20th–21st LONG-HEM	Routine Work	
" 22nd AIRE	Evacuated 31 horses.	
" 23rd LONGHEM	Routine work	
" 24th " "	Marched from LONGHEM to ST MARIE at billets at 7.30 on 25th. by night arriving	
25th ST MARIE CAPPELL	Went to HARZEBROUCK to inquire re evacuating horses from that Railhead but was informed they could not do so owing to detrained up to 2000	
" 26th " "	Received orders from ADV.S. & Ind. Cav Div to Evacuate from CAESTRE RAILHEAD. Evacuated 19 horses from AIRE before above orders were received.	
" 27th " "	Routine work	
" 28th " "	Section marched with B Echelon of the brigade to the

WAR DIARY
or
INTELLIGENCE SUMMARY.

Army Form C. 2118.

Hour, Date, Place.	Summary of Events and Information.	Remarks and references to Appendices.
5 pm. 29th JAN. 1.2 BIZET	Village of MARIE CAPPELL; transport was parked here for the night.	
30th	Marched from MARIE CAPPELL to BIZET. Routine work.	

R. A. Goodruff. Capt. AVC.
O.C. Mobile Veterinary Section
Lucknow Cavalry Brigade.

Serial No. 178.

121/5799

WAR DIARY
OF
Mobile Veterinary Section, Lucknow Cavalry Brigade.

From 1st May 1915 TO 31st May 1915.

WAR DIARY
or
INTELLIGENCE SUMMARY

(Erase heading not required.)

Army Form C. 2118.

Instructions regarding War Diaries and Intelligence Summaries are contained in F. S. Regs., Part II, and the Staff Manual respectively. Title pages will be prepared in manuscript.

A.G.'s OFFICE AT THE BASE
3 JUN. 1915
INDIAN SECTION

Hour, Date, Place.	Summary of Events and Information.	Remarks and references to Appendices.
May 1st 1915. CAESTRE	Received orders from ADVS 1st Ind Cavalry Division to move my section from S.JANS-CLER-BIEZEN to CAESTRE Railhead. Marched at 11 am. Arrived CAESTRE at 3.30pm. Billeted 1/4 mile from station. Drew rations from Railhead. Could not draw rations for Indians.	
2nd " "	DDVS 1st Indian Cavalry Corps applied HQ 2nd Army for permission to remain in billet, as I belonged to 1st Cavalry Bde, British Forces.	
3rd " "	Received permission to remain in billet, but British Cavalry returned so gave up billet. Marched to S. SYLVESTRE (CAPPEL) & billeted.	
4th S.SYLVESTRE	Received horses from 1st & 2nd Indian Cavalry Divisions. Collecting horses left behind by brigades around WATOU area.	
5th " "	Collecting horses left behind at HOUTKERQUE, STAPLE, & CASSEL district. Evacuating horses from CAESTRE Railhead.	
9th " "	Marched section to AIRE RAILHEAD & billeted at NEUF PRE, relieving the MVS. SECUNDERABAD CAVALRY BRIGADE.	

Army Form C. 2118.

WAR DIARY
or
INTELLIGENCE SUMMARY.
(Erase heading not required.)

Instructions regarding War Diaries and Intelligence Summaries are contained in F. S. Regs., Part II, and the Staff Manual respectively. Title pages will be prepared in manuscript.

Hour, Date, Place.	Summary of Events and Information.	Remarks and references to Appendices.
9th to 26th NEUFPRÉ	Admitting sick horses from both divisions. Evacuating from AIRE to ABBEVILLE.	
27th LONGUECROIX	Marched section from railhead joined up brigade at LONGUE CROIX	
28th ERKELSBRUGGE	Marched with B Echelon of the brigade to ERKELSBRUGGE.	
29th to 31st " "	Admitting + treating sick horses of the brigade.	

Army Form C. 2118.

WAR DIARY
or
INTELLIGENCE SUMMARY.
(Erase heading not required.)

Instructions regarding War Diaries and Intelligence Summaries are contained in F. S. Regs., Part II, and the Staff Manual respectively. Title pages will be prepared in manuscript.

Hour, Date, Place.	Summary of Events and Information.	Remarks and references to Appendices.
11 P.M. 12-9-15 ST. Gratien	M.V.S marched to BEAUCOURT & there met-led horse party & returned with it to ST. LEGER arriving 7.30 a.m.	
7.30 A.M. 13-9-15 ST. LEGER	moved into new billets.	
15-9-15 " "	Ordinary Routine Work.	
21-9-15 " "	Evacuated twenty seven horses from railhead LONGPRÉ to No 5 Veterinary Hospital, Abbeville.	
2 P.M. 22-9-15 " "	By orders of Brigade, the mobile Veterinary Section left ST. LEGER & marched to Monte PLASIR.	
5 P.M. " " "	Moved into new billets at LE QUESNEL FERME.	

Army Form C. 2118.

WAR DIARY
or
INTELLIGENCE SUMMARY.
(Erase heading not required.)

Hour, Date, Place.	Summary of Events and Information.	Remarks and references to Appendices.
23-9-15. MONTE PLAISIR	Evacuated twenty seven horses from railhead DOULLENS to No 5 Veterinary Hospital, Abbeville.	
24-9-15 " "	Evacuated thirteen sick horses to No 5 Vety Hospital Abbeville.	
26-9-15 " "	Evacuated thirty horses from railhead DOULLENS to No 5 Veterinary Hospital Abbeville.	
28-9-15 " "	Evacuated seven horses to Hospital Abbeville.	
29-9-15 " "	Evacuated one pneumonia case to Hospital Abbeville.	
30-9-15 " "	Collected one horse left behind by K.D.G. at ST. LEGER. which was suffering from strained fetlock & unable to march.	

Army Form C. 2118.

WAR DIARY
or
INTELLIGENCE SUMMARY.

(Erase heading not required.)

Instructions regarding War Diaries and Intelligence Summaries are contained in F. S. Regs., Part II, and the Staff Manual respectively. Title pages will be prepared in manuscript.

Hour, Date, Place.	Summary of Events and Information.	Remarks and references to Appendices.
30-9-15 MONT PLASIR	Evacuated three horses to hospital, Attinville.	

W.E. Clipper
Lieut AVC
O.C. Mobile Veterinary Section
Lucknow Cavalry Bde

Army Form C. 2118.

WAR DIARY
or
INTELLIGENCE SUMMARY.

(Erase heading not required.)

Hour, Date, Place.	Summary of Events and Information.	Remarks and references to Appendices.
1-10-15 MONT PLAISIR	Evacuated eight horses to No 5 Veterinary Hospital Abbeville from railhead DOULLENS.	
2-10-15 " "	Ordinary Routine Work	
3-10-15 " "	Evacuated thirty eight horses (Cart by D.A.D.R.) to No 5 Veterinary Hospital Abbeville. Also 5 sick horses	
6-10-15 " "	Evacuated eighteen sick horses to No 5 Veterinary Hospital Abbeville from railhead, DOULLENS.	
8-10-15 " "	Evacuated seventeen sick horses to No 5 Veterinary Hospital Abbeville from railhead DOULLENS	
11-10-15 " "	Evacuated nineteen horses to No 5 Veterinary Hospital Abbeville.	

WAR DIARY or INTELLIGENCE SUMMARY.

Army Form C. 2118.

(Erase heading not required.)

Hour, Date, Place.	Summary of Events and Information.	Remarks and references to Appendices.
14-10-15 Mont Plaisir	Evacuated ten horses from sickbed Double NS to No 5 Veterinary Hospital, Abbeville	
18-10-15 "	Evacuated nine horses East by D.A.D.V.	
18-10-15 "	Evacuated seventeen sick horses to No 5 Veterinary Hospital	
21-10-15 "	Evacuated fourteen sick horses to Abbeville	
21-10-15 "	Received Orders from Brigade for M.V.S. to march to CAVILLON on 22nd	
6.AM. 22-10-15 "	Marched to CAVILLON & took over new billets there.	
11.AM. 25-10-15 Cavillon	By orders of Division the Mobile Section marched to HANGEST & took over new billets in Richecourt FERME.	

SERIAL NO. 178.

Confidential

War Diary

of

Mobile Veterinary Section Lucknow Cavalry Brigade

FROM 1st January 1918 TO 31st January 1918

Army Form C. 2118.

WAR DIARY
or
INTELLIGENCE SUMMARY.
(Erase heading not required.)

Instructions regarding War Diaries and Intelligence Summaries are contained in F. S. Regs., Part II. and the Staff Manual respectively. Title pages will be prepared in manuscript.

Place	Date	Hour	Summary of Events and Information	Remarks and references to Appendices
FIREVILLES	1-1-16		Ordinary Routine Work - SE No 982. Corporal E King A.V.C. promoted to Sergeant -	
	2-1-16		Orders received from A.D.V.S. that all horses in contact with Mange Cases from 1-1-16 to be dressed with hot Calcium Sulphide.	
"	4-1-16		No 22 Veterinary Hospital ABBEVILLE now opened as Reception Hospital	
"	"		Evacuated 6 horses to No 22 Veterinary Hospital	
"	7-1-16		Evacuated 10 horses to No 22 Hospital	
"	9-1-16		Tested all horses & mules on strength of Mobile Veterinary Section with Mallein (Eye method)	
"	10-1-16		Two horses reacted to Mallein Test & were destroyed. P.M. showed extensive lesions in the lungs of one horse - The other horse showed no lesions on examination	
"	11-1-16		Eight horses evacuated to No 22 Veterinary Hospital	
"	15-1-16		Ordinary Routine Work	
"	20-1-16		Evacuated 8 horses to No 22 Vety Hospital	
"	26-1-16		Evacuated 4 horses to No 22 Vety Hospital	
"	31-1-16		Ordinary Routine Work	

W.E. Phipps Lieut A.V.C.
O.C. Mobile Veterinary Section
Lucknow Cav Bde

SERIAL NO. 178.

Confidential

War Diary

of

Mobile Veterinary Section, Lucknow Cavalry Brigade.

FROM 1st February 1916 TO 29th February 1916

Army Form C. 2118.

WAR DIARY
or
INTELLIGENCE SUMMARY.
(Erase heading not required.)

Instructions regarding War Diaries and Intelligence Summaries are contained in F.S. Regs., Part II. and the Staff Manual respectively. Title pages will be prepared in manuscript.

MOBILE VETERINARY SECTION
LUCKNOW CAVALRY BDE.
No. 421
Date 4/3/16

6 MAR 1916

Place	Date	Hour	Summary of Events and Information	Remarks and references to Appendices
FRIEVILLERS	1-2-16		Ordinary Routine Work. Evacuated five horses to No 22 Vety Hospital, ABBEVILLE.	
"	8-2-16		SE. No 962 Sergeant. E. KING. A.V.C. despatched from this Unit to join No 7 Veterinary Hospital.	
"	9-2-16		Evacuated eleven horses to No 22 Veterinary Hospital.	
"	12-2-16		Ordinary Routine Work.	
"	17-2-16		Evacuated 7 horses cast by D.A.D.R.	
"	19-2-16		Evacuated twenty three horses to No 22 Veterinary Hospital (nineteen of these horses were cast by D.A.D.R.)	
"	29-2-16		Ordinary Routine Work.	

W.E. Phipps Lieut
O.C. Mobile Veterinary Section
Lucknow Cavalry Bde

SERIAL NO. 118.

Confidential

War Diary

of

Mobile Veterinary Section, Lucknow Cavalry Brigade.

FROM 1st March 1916 TO 31st March 1916.

Army Form C. 2118.

WAR DIARY
or
INTELLIGENCE SUMMARY.

(Erase heading not required.)

Instructions regarding War Diaries and Intelligence Summaries are contained in F. S. Regs., Part II, and the Staff Manual respectively. Title pages will be prepared in manuscript.

Hour, Date, Place.	Summary of Events and Information.	Remarks and references to Appendices.
29-10-15 HANGEST	Evacuated nine horses to No 5 Veterinary Hospital Abbeville from railhead LONG-PRE	
31-10-15 "	Evacuated three horses to Abbeville	

W. E. Phipps
Lieutenant
OC mobile Veterinary Section
Lucknow Cavalry Bde.

SERIAL NO. 178.

Confidential

War Diary

of

Mobile Veterinary Section, Lucknow Cavalry Brigade.

FROM 1st November 1915 TO (0) 31st December 1915.

Army Form C. 2118.

WAR DIARY
or
INTELLIGENCE SUMMARY.
(Erase heading not required.)

Hour, Date, Place.	Summary of Events and Information.	Remarks and references to Appendices.
1-11-15 HANGEST	Ordinary Routine Work. Evacuated four horses to Abbeville.	
5-11-15 "	By Orders of Division Mobile Veterinary Section marched to LE QUESNOT & took over new billets there. Village to north HANGEST, & occupied by 17th Lancers. Village to South PICQUENEY occupied by 29th Lancers. & Lucknow 2d Ambulance.	
5-11-15 LE QUESNOT	Evacuated five horses to Abbeville.	
6-11-15 " "	Evacuated twelve horses to Abbeville.	
12-11-15 " "	Evacuated sixteen horses to Abbeville.	

WAR DIARY or INTELLIGENCE SUMMARY

Army Form C. 2118.

Place	Date	Hour	Summary of Events and Information	Remarks and references to Appendices
LE QUESNOT	16-11-15		Evacuated 5 horses to No 5 Veterinary Hospital Abbeville.	
"	18-11-15	1.30 PM	Under orders from Lucknow Cav Brigade the Mobile Veterinary Section marched to LE CATELET and took over new billets there. Two troops of 15th Squadron K.D. Gds occupies other half of village, while is only 2 Kilomètres from railed LONGPRE. Longpre being occupied by K.D. Gds.	
LE CATELET	26-11-15		Ordinary Routine Work.	
	26-11-15		Evacuated thirteen sick horses to No 5 Veterinary Hospital.	
	27-11-15		Ordinary Routine Work	
	2-12-15		Evacuated seven sick horses to No 5 Veterinary Hospital.	
	7-12-15		Evacuated five sick horses to No 5 Vet'y Hospital.	
	12-12-15		By orders of D.V.S. all horses to be tested for glanders with mallein. The palpebral method to be adopted.	
	14-12-15		No. 5 Vet'y Hospital Abbeville closed for receiving sick horses. No 14 Vet'y Hospital Abbeville now to be used instead.	
	14-12-15		Evacuated fourteen horses to No 14 Vet'n Hospital reception hospital	

Army Form C. 2118.

Instructions regarding War Diaries and Intelligence Summaries are contained in F.S. Regs., Part II. and the Staff Manual respectively. Title pages will be prepared in manuscript.

WAR DIARY
or
INTELLIGENCE SUMMARY.
(Erase heading not required.)

Place	Date	Hour	Summary of Events and Information	Remarks and references to Appendices
LE CATELET	15.12.15	10 A.M.	By order from Brigade the Mobile Veterinary Section marched from LE CATELET to FRIREULLES. (about 13 kilometers from ABBEVILLE and on the DIEPPE – ABBEVILLE Road) a took over new billets here. "B" Squadron 36 Jacob Horse occupies the other part of village. Ordinary Routine Work.	
FRIREULLES	16.12.15			
	20.12.15		Evacuated five horses to No 14 Veterinary Hospital Abbeville sick, all horses which are likely to take more than eight days to recover are to be evacuated.	
	22.12.15		By order of D.D.V.S. J.E.F. memo No A-3534 J.E.F. Horses suffering from mange evacuated to Base will be returned to the Corps when cured provided that when evacuated they are properly labelled. After receipt by Remount Department Abbeville the animals will be sent to the Corps Field Remount Section & reissued to units as required.	
	24.12.15			

1577 Wt.W10791/1773 500,000 1/15 D. D. & L.   A.D.S.S./Forms/C. 2118.

WAR DIARY or INTELLIGENCE SUMMARY

Army Form C. 2118.

Place	Date	Hour	Summary of Events and Information	Remarks and references to Appendices
FRIREVILLES	24/12/15		Evacuated 3 horses to Abbeville	
	29.12.15		Evacuated 5 horses to Abbeville	
	30.12.15		Evacuated 1 horse to Abbeville.	

Mr E Phipps Lieutenant SR
O.C.
Mobile Veterinary Section
Jackson Cavalry Bde.

Army Form C. 2118.

WAR DIARY
or
INTELLIGENCE SUMMARY.
(Erase heading not required.)

Instructions regarding War Diaries and Intelligence Summaries are contained in F. S. Regs., Part II. and the Staff Manual respectively. Title pages will be prepared in manuscript.

MOBILE VETERINARY SECTION
No. 517
Date March '16
LUCKNOW CAVALRY BDE

Place	Date	Hour	Summary of Events and Information	Remarks and references to Appendices
FRIREULLES	1-3-16		Ordinary Routine Work	
	5-3-16		Evacuated ten horses to No 22 Veterinary Hospital Abbeville	
	6-3-16		Evacuated by Motor Ambulance (sling from No 22 Vety. Hospital) one horse of R.D. Dns with injured shoulder	
	20-3-16		Evacuated seven horses to No 22 Vety Hospital	
	23-3-16		Evacuated five horses to " "	
	24-3-16	9-30am	Evacuated five horses to " "	
	25-3-16	9-30am	G.O.C. Lucknow Cavalry Brigade inspected all horses of the Section	
	26-3-16	8-30am	Under orders from the Lucknow Cav Bde the Mobile Vety Section marched from FRIREULLES to CUMONVILLE and took over new billets there. CUMONVILLE situated about 20 Kilometres N.E. of ABBEVILLE and about 4 Kilometres N.W. of AUXI-LE-CHATEAU. Kings Dragoon Guards occupying GUESCHART about one Kilometre	

WAR DIARY
or
INTELLIGENCE SUMMARY.

(Erase heading not required.)

Army Form C. 2118.

Place	Date	Hour	Summary of Events and Information	Remarks and references to Appendices
CUMONVILLE	30-7-16		W. of CUMONVILLE. No other proof hibitted of CUMONVILLE 6 others received from 12th Indian Cavalry Division that all horses to be picketed out of doors - no stables or sheds to be occupied without further orders. This area was previously occupied by French troops and cases of mange amongst glanders those occupied among their horses.	
"		3.30 PM	Evacuated by rail from No. 22 Veterinary Hospital eight horses to AUXI-LE-CHATEAU (Authors) G.O.C. Lucknow Cavalry Brigade inspected billets taken over by Mobile Veterinary Section.	

W.T. Phipps Capt
Cmdg.
Mob'g Veterinary Section
Lucknow Cavalry Brigade

SERIAL NO. 178

Confidential

War Diary

of

Mobile Veterinary Section, Lucknow Cavalry Brigade

FROM 1st April 1916 TO 30th April 1916.

Army Form C. 2118.

WAR DIARY
or
INTELLIGENCE SUMMARY.
(Erase heading not required.)

Instructions regarding War Diaries and Intelligence Summaries are contained in F. S. Regs., Part II. and the Staff Manual respectively. Title pages will be prepared in manuscript.

Place	Date	Hour	Summary of Events and Information	Remarks and references to Appendices
DUMONVILLE	1-4-16		Ordinary Routine Work	
	3-4-16		Evacuated by road, four sick horses to No 22 Veterinary Hospital, ABBEVILLE	
	5-4-16		Evacuated by road, nine sick horses to " "	
	16-4-16		Evacuated from railhead AUXI LE CHATEAU. eleven sick horses to No 22 Veterinary Hospital, ABBEVILLE	
	19-4-16		Evacuated by road, ten sick horses to No 22 Veterinary Hospital Auxi: LE CHATEAU.	
	21-4-16		Evacuated five horses from railhead No 22 Veterinary Hospital	
	25-4-16		Evacuated by road fifteen horses to No 22 Veterinary Hospital	
	28-4-16		Evacuated by road, nine horses " "	
	30-4-16		Received orders from Brigade Major to march on the following day with "B" Echelon of Brigade to ST. RIQUER. (Training Area)	

W.E. Chipp Capt
O.C. Jackson Mobile Veterinary Section

SERIAL NO. 178.

Confidential

War Diary

of

Mobile Veterinary Section, Lucknow Cavalry Brigade

FROM 1st May 1916 TO 31st May 1916.

Army Form C. 2118.

WAR DIARY
or
INTELLIGENCE SUMMARY.
(Erase heading not required.)

Instructions regarding War Diaries and Intelligence Summaries are contained in F.S. Regs., Part II. and the Staff Manual respectively. Title pages will be prepared in manuscript.

Place	Date	Hour	Summary of Events and Information	Remarks and references to Appendices
CUMONVILLE	1-5-16	10 AM	Under orders from Lucknow Cavalry Bde. Mobile Vety Section marched with "B" Echelon of Bde. to ST. RIQUER (Divisional Training Area) & took over Billets there. King's Dragoon Guards - two Squadrons of Jodhpur Lancers - 36 Jacobs Horse + Bde Head Quarters occupying same village	
"	1-5-16		Evacuated from CUMONVILLE by road, fourteen sick horses to No 22 Veterinary Hospital ABBEVILLE. Conducting party afterwards marching to New area and joining Mobile Section there.	
ST. RIQUER	3-5-16		Indian Personnel under the Brigade Veterinary Officer formed a First Aid + Collecting party on Divisional Scheme - No casualties recorded	
"	4-5-16		Indian Personnel under B.V.O. formed First Aid + Collecting party on Divisional Scheme	
"	5-5-16		Indian Personnel under B.V.O. carried out same scheme as previous day	

1577 Wt.W10791/1773 500,000 1/15 D.D. & L.   A.D.S.S./Form/C. 2118.

WAR DIARY or INTELLIGENCE SUMMARY

Army Form C. 2118.

Place	Date	Hour	Summary of Events and Information	Remarks and references to Appendices
ST RIQUIER	6-5-16		Two horses evacuated by road to No 22 Veterinary Hospital ABBEVILLE.	
	7-5-16		Evacuated two horses to No 22 Veterinary Hospital ABBEVILLE.	
	9-5-16		Under orders from Lucknow Cavalry Bde the Mobile Section marched independently to CUMONVILLE & took over previous billets.	
CUMONVILLE	9-5-16		Evacuated eleven sick horses from suitable A/71. LE CHATEAU to No 22 Veterinary Hospital ABBEVILLE.	
	10-5-16		Under Brigade orders the Mobile Vety Section marched with "B" Echelon to HONVAL & took over new billets there - The Lucknow Machine Gun Squadron also occupying this area. HONVAL situated about four kilometers N.E of FREVENT (LENS MAP). Kings Dragoon Gds occupying SERICOURT N.W of HONVAL 29 Lancers occupying CANETTEMONT. E of HONVAL Bde H.Q + Jodhpur Lancers occupying REBREUVE S of Honval.	

WAR DIARY or INTELLIGENCE SUMMARY

Army Form C. 2118.

Place	Date	Hour	Summary of Events and Information	Remarks and references to Appendices
HONVAL	12.5.16		Ordinary Routine Work.	
"	15.5.16		Evacuated thirteen sick horses from railhead FREVENT to No 22 Veterinary Hospital ABBEVILLE.	
"	18.5.16		Evacuated by rail twelve horses to No 22 Veterinary Hospital.	
"	25.5.16	11 AM	Inspection of the Mobile Veterinary Section by the Commander in Chief.	
"	26.5.16		Evacuated fourteen sick horses from railhead FREVENT to No 22 Veterinary Hospital.	
"	30.5.16		Evacuated eighteen sick horses to No 22 Veterinary Hospital by rail.	

W. Phipp Capt
Cmdg 2nd Indian Mobile Veterinary Section

SERIAL NO. 178.

Confidential War Diary of

Mobile Veterinary Section, Lucknow Cavalry Brigade.

FROM 1st June 1916 TO 30th June 1916.

Army Form C. 2118.

WAR DIARY
or
INTELLIGENCE SUMMARY.
(Erase heading not required.)

Instructions regarding War Diaries and Intelligence Summaries are contained in F. S. Regs., Part II. and the Staff Manual respectively. Title pages will be prepared in manuscript.

Place	Date	Hour	Summary of Events and Information	Remarks and references to Appendices
HONVAL	1/6/16		Ordinary Routine Work.	
"	4/6/16		Evacuated thirteen horses to No 22 Veterinary Hospital	
"	7/6/16		" seven horses to " " "	
"	10/6/16		" eight horses to " " "	
"	13/6/16		" four horses to " " "	
"	17/6/16		" eight horses to " " "	
"	21/6/16		" forty three horses to " " "	
"	23/6/16		(Thirty seven of these horses were cast by D.D.V. Third Army) Evacuated two mange cases + one injured horse (by motor Ambulance) to No 22 Veterinary Hospital.	
"	24/6/16		Evacuated ten sick horses to No 22 Veterinary Hospital.	
"	25/6/16		" ten sick horses " " " "	
"	30/6/16		Under orders from Lucknow Cav Bde the mobile Veterinary Section marched with Brigade to GROUCHES. + took over new billets there. CROUCHES is situate about 4½ Kilometres N.E. of DOULLENS. Brigade Head Quarters + Kings Dragoon Guards also	

Army Form C. 2118.

WAR DIARY
or
INTELLIGENCE SUMMARY.
(Erase heading not required.)

Place	Date	Hour	Summary of Events and Information	Remarks and references to Appendices
GROUCHES	30/6/16		Billeted in the village. 29th Lancers occupying MILLY on the LUCHEUX-DOULLENS road. 36 Jacobs Horse occupying BOUT DES PRES. between MILLY & GROUCHES.	

W.T. Clipp? Capt AVC.
OC Lucknow Mobile Veterinary Section.

1/7/16

SERIAL NO. 178.

Confidential
War Diary
of

Mobile Veterinary Section, Lucknow Cavalry Brigade.

FROM 1st July 1916 TO 31st July 1916.

Confidential

War Diary
of
Lucknow Cavalry Mobile Vety section

From 1st July 1916 To 31st July 1916.

WAR DIARY or INTELLIGENCE SUMMARY

Army Form C. 2118.

Place	Date	Hour	Summary of Events and Information	Remarks and references to Appendices
GROUCHES	1.7.16		Ordinary Routine Work	
"	2.7.16		Under orders from Brigade the Mobile Veterinary Section marched with Brigade & took over billets at FROHEN.LE.GRAND. FROHEN.LE.GRAND situated about 15 Kilometres N.W. of GROUCHES and on AUXI.LE.CHATEAU – DOULLENS Road. Brigade Head Quarters and King's Dragoon Guards occupying the same village. 29 Lancers + 36 Jacob's Horse occupying VILLERS L'HÔPITAL	
FROHEN LE GRAND	4.7.16		Ordinary Routine Work	
"	6.7.16		Evacuated twelve sick horses from GARE BOUQUE MAISON - also two mange case by road to No 22 Veterinary Hospital ABBEVILLE.	
"	11.7.16		Evacuated 23 sick horses from BOUQUE MAISON by train to No 22 Veterinary Hospital ABBEVILLE.	
"	14.7.16		Evacuated two mange cases to No 22 Veterinary Hospital (marched by road).	
"	15.7.16		Evacuated ten sick horses by train from BOUQUE MAISON to No. 22 Veterinary Hospital	

WAR DIARY or INTELLIGENCE SUMMARY

Army Form C. 2118.

(Erase heading not required.)

Place	Date	Hour	Summary of Events and Information	Remarks and references to Appendices
FROHEN LE GRAND	18.7.16		Evacuated by train from BOUQUE MAISON eighteen sick horses to No 22 Veterinary Hospital.	
"	19.7.16		Under orders from Brigade the mobile Veterinary Section marched with B Echelon under R.T.O to new area + took over billets at VILLERS BRULIN. Brigade Head Quarters + Brigade Horse occupying the same village. VILLERS BRULIN Situate about twenty Kilometres N.W of ARRAS and about four kilometres from AUBIGNY (LENS Map) Lucknow Machine Gun Squadron occupying BETHENCOURT.	
VILLERS BRULIN.	22.7.16		The mobile Veterinary Section moved from VILLERS BRULIN and took over billets at BETHENCOURT.	
BETHEN-COURT	23.7.16		No.458 Sergeant Ribbins, F.C. (AVC) promoted to P/A. Staff Sergeant from 30 June 1916 & transferred from Lucknow M.V.S to No 19 Veterinary Hospital on 23/7/16, for duty.	
"	25.7.16		No 651 Sergeant Perrin. W.(AVC) joined from No 4 Veterinary Hospital for duty.	

Army Form C. 2118.

954
3/7/16

WAR DIARY
or
INTELLIGENCE SUMMARY

(Erase heading not required.)

Instructions regarding War Diaries and Intelligence Summaries are contained in F. S. Regs., Part II. and the Staff Manual respectively. Title Pages will be prepared in manuscript.

Place	Date	Hour	Summary of Events and Information	Remarks and references to Appendices
BETHEN- COURT	25/7/16		Evacuated twenty four sick & cast horses from railhead TINQUES to No 22 Veterinary Hospital	
"	30/7/16		Several cases of mange have lately occurred in the Brigade, notably in 36th Jacobs Horse and 29 Lancers. As G.O.C. Division will not sanction the evacuation of these horses Mobile Veterinary Section is ordered to dress them once weekly with hot calcium sulphide solution. The facilities for this treatment, which has been carried on for some time, seems inadequate to cope with the disease which is on the increase. A.D.V.S informed and G.O.C. Brigade informed of the number of cases & the measures taken to check the spread of the disease	
	31/7/16		Evacuated seven sick horses from railhead TINQUES to No 22 Veterinary Hospital	

W.E. Phipps Capt.
Commanding
Mobile Veterinary Section
Lucknow Cavalry Brigade

31/7/16

SERIAL NO. 176.

Confidential

War Diary

of

Mobile Veterinary Section, Lucknow Cavalry Brigade.

FROM 1st August 1916 TO 31st August 1916

Army Form C. 2118.

WAR DIARY
or
INTELLIGENCE SUMMARY.
(Erase heading not required.)

Place	Date	Hour	Summary of Events and Information	Remarks and references to Appendices
BETHENCOURT	1.8/16		Ordinary Routine Work. WSC	
"	6.8/16		Evacuated twenty sick horses from railhead TINQUES to No 22 Veterinary Hospital. ABBEVILLE. WSC	
"	8.8/16		Evacuated twenty three horses from railhead TINQUES to No 22. Veterinary Hospital.	
"	9/16		Under orders from Brigade the Mobile Veterinary Section moved with Bde Head Quarters Signal Troop to PAS + took over new billets at HURTBISE F^m. PAS situated about ten kilometres E of DOULLENS (LENS map) VII Corps H.Q at Chateau PAS. Lucknow Mobile Veterinary Section at HURTBISE F^m just W of FAMECHON. WSC	
HURTBISE F^m	10.8/16		Ordinary Routine Work WSC	
"	12.8/16		Evacuated Six Mange Cases (Kings Dragoon Gds) from railhead SAULTY to No 22 Vety Hospital WSC	

WAR DIARY or INTELLIGENCE SUMMARY

Lucknow Cav Bde
Mobile Vety Section
Lucknow Cavalry Bde.

Army Form C. 2118.

Place	Date	Hour	Summary of Events and Information	Remarks and references to Appendices
HURTBISE Fm	16/8/16		Evacuated twenty six horses to No 2 2 Veterinary Mobile from sickhead SAUTY. W.R.B.	
	18/8/16		Handed over command of Mobile Veterinary Section to Capt P.D. Carey. W.R.C	
	18/8/16		Took over Command of M.V.S. from Capt Phipps. P.DC	
	19/8/16		Inspected 36 yards Horse with A.D.V.S. from the Govern. P.DC	
	20/8/16		Burnt 44 Suspicious mange Cases in Section field. C.D.C Section throws Break a very firm, muddy lot. Two undiagnosis. Second Season	
	21/8/16		Marched the Section to COUTURELLE. P.DC	
	22/8/16		Evacuated 11 Sick horse to No 22 V.H. P.DC	
	27/8/16		Evacuated 7 Sick horses to Chair V.H. P.DC	
	29/8/16		Brigadier General inspected Section. P.DC	

The horses in this division are all shod with a width to toe shoe. This shoe is going in Hurry + should also be most satisfactory if made made in those units that came British Sunning Smiths, the shoes are well made but the shoe as made by Indian Artificers is [illegible] bad in every way. The Foot Surfaces of the shoe is never even, it is never turned up sufficiently to be of any use, I have seen to many coin B[urning] SSn of coinng by this shoe to be able to recommend its use except in Units will skilled workmen in if I wound from Ordnance our unit contention that Hay & Canely seems the most dif' sufficiently to obtain the best results in turning out the Shoe.

31/8/16

P.P. Carey. Capt MC
O.C. Lucknow Cav. Bde
Mobile Vet Section.

SERIAL NO. 118.

Confidential

War Diary

of

.........MOBILE VETERINARY SECTION, LUCKNOW CAVALRY BRIGADE..........

FROM 1st SEPTEMBER........, 1916 TO 30th SEPTEMBER......, 1916

WAR DIARY or INTELLIGENCE SUMMARY

Army Form C. 2118.

(Erase heading not required.)

Instructions regarding War Diaries and Intelligence Summaries are contained in F. S. Regs., Part II. and the Staff Manual respectively. Title Pages will be prepared in manuscript.

MOBILE VETERINARY No. 1167 Date 2-x-16 LUCKNOW CAVALRY B.DE

Place	Date	Hour	Summary of Events and Information	Remarks and references to Appendices
COUTURELLE	1-9-16		Ordinary Routine work.	
"	3-9-16		Under orders received from Lucknow Cavalry Brigade Headquarters the Mobile Veterinary Section marched with Brigade to Occoches and occupied new billets there.	
OCCOCHE'S	4-9-16		Under orders received from L.C.B. H.Q. the M.V.S. marched to BRAILLY CORNEHOTTE and took over front billets and machine gun & photom occupying billets in same village. L.C.B. Headquarters and Lucknow	
BRAILLY-CORN -EHOTTE	5-9-16		Ordinary routine work.	
"	8-9-16		Evacuated eight sick horses by rail from ST. RIQUIER to No 32 Veterinary hospital ABBEVILLE. Evacuated six sick horses by road from BRAILLY to No 22 Vety Hospital ABBEVILLE	
"	10-9-16		Evacuated one sick horse by Motor Ambulance from BRAILLY to No 22 Vety Ho. "	
"	11-9-16	10-30am	Under orders received from L.C.B. H.Q. the M.V.S. marched to FROHEN-LE-GRAND took over billets there as in July 1916	
FROHEN-LE-GRAND	12-9-16		Under orders received from L.C.B. N.Q. the M.V.S. marched to HEM and took over new billets there	
"	13-9-16		Evacuated 29 sick horses from BOUQUE MAISON by rail to No 22 V.H. ABBEVILLE. Under orders received from L.C.B. H.Q. the M.V.S. marched with "B" Echelon of Brigade to a camp in the South Army area situated near ALLONVILLE. Evacuated 5 sick horses from BOUQUE MAISON by rail to No 22 V.H. ABBEVILLE	
ALLONVILLE CAMP	14-9-16		Evacuated 14 sick horses from FRECHENCOURT by rail to No 7 Vety Hospital FORGES-LES -EAUX	
"	15-9-16	4-30am	Under orders received from L.C.B. H.Q. the M.V.S. marched in rear of "A" Echelon of Brigade to a camp situated near MORLANCOURT	
"	16-9-16		Evacuated 21 sick horses from MERICOURT to No 7 V.H., FORGES-LES-EAUX.	

WAR DIARY or INTELLIGENCE SUMMARY

Army Form C. 2118.

(Erase heading not required.)

Place	Date	Hour	Summary of Events and Information	Remarks and references to Appendices
MORLANCOURT CAMP	19-9-16		Evacuated 16 sick horses from EDGE HILL by rail to No 7 V.H. FORGES-LES-EAUX	
"	22-9-16		Evacuated 18 sick horses from EDGE HILL " " " "	
"	25-9-16		Evacuated 24 sick horses from GROVE TOWN " " " "	
"	26-9-16		Under orders received from L.C.B., H.Q., the M.V.S. marched with Brigade to a camp in MAMETZ	
MAMETZ	27-9-16		Under orders received from L.C.B., H.Q., the M.V.S. marched to a camp near BUSSY-LES-DAOURS	
BUSSY-LES-DAOURS	28-9-16		Left 4 wounded horses at Collecting Station A.V.C. at MÉAULTE. Under orders received from L.C.B, H.Q, the M.V.S. marched to a camp at HANGEST-SUR-SOMME. Evacuated 4 sick horses by rail from CORBIE to No 7 Vety. Hospital FORGES-LES-EAUX	
HANGEST-SUR-SOMME	29-9-16		3 " " " " " HANGEST-SUR-SOMME to No 7 V.H. " " Under orders received from L.C.B., H.Q., the M.V.S. marched with "A" Echelon of Brigade to MONTFLIERS and took over new billets there	
MONTFLIERS	30-9-16		Under orders from L.C.B., H.Q., the M.V.S. marched to GRÉCY and took over billets at the Saw Mills	

P. B. Corey - Capt.
Commanding
Lucknow Mobile Vety. Section

SERIAL NO. 178.

Confidential
War Diary
of

Mobile Veterinary Section, Lucknow Cavalry Brigade.

FROM 1st October 1916 TO 30th November 1916
          31st October

WAR DIARY
or
INTELLIGENCE SUMMARY

(Erase heading not required.)

Army Form C. 2118.

Place	Date	Hour	Summary of Events and Information	Remarks and references to Appendices
CRECY	1-X-16		Veterinary Routine Work	
"	3-X-16		Evacuated Veterinary Hospital and sent invalid to No 2 Vety. Hospital ABBEVILLE	
"	8-X-16		Evacuated mules and cast animals to No 2 Vety Hospital ABBEVILLE by road	
"	9-X-16		Evacuated mules and cast horses to No 2 Vety Hospital ABBEVILLE	
"	10-X-16		Evacuated mules and cast horses by road to No 2 Vety Hospital ABBEVILLE	
"	11-X-16		Evacuated mules and horses by road to No 2 Vety Hospital ABBEVILLE.	
"	12-X-16		Evacuated mules and horses by road to No 2 Vety Hospital ABBEVILLE	
"	13-X-16		M.V.S. was inspected by D.D.V.S., Cavalry Corps	
"	14-X-16		Evacuated cast mules and horses by road to No 2 Vety. Hospital	
"	16-X-16		Evacuated one cast horse by road to No 2 Vety. Hospital	
"	19-X-16		Evacuated cast mules and horses by road to No 2 Vety Hospital	
"	20-X-16		Evacuated cast mules and horses by road to No 2 Vety Hospital	
"	25-X-16		Evacuated cast horses from FOREST-MONTIERS to No 2 Vety Hospital	
"	27-X-16		Evacuated cast horses by road to No 2 Vety Hospital	
"	30-X-16		Evacuated one cast horse by road to No 2 Vety Hospital	
"	31-X-16		Evacuated horse from MACHY in an ambulance van to No 2 Vety Hospital	

(P.B. Caray)
Capt. A.V.C.
Commanding
M.V.S., Lucknow Cavalry Brigade

SECRET

WAR DIARY

OF

LUCKNOW BDE M.V.S. 4TH CAV. DIVN.

Nov. 1st to 30th, 1916.

Army Form C. 2118.

WAR DIARY
or
INTELLIGENCE SUMMARY
(Erase heading not required.)

Instructions regarding War Diaries and Intelligence Summaries are contained in F. S. Regs., Part II. and the Staff Manual respectively. Title Pages will be prepared in manuscript.

Place	Date	Hour	Summary of Events and Information	Remarks and references to Appendices
CRECY	1.11.16		Escorted six sick horses by road to No 2 Veterinary Hospital ABBEVILLE	
	3.11.16		Under orders received from Staff, split Unit into two Brigades to work the M V S.	
HYMMEVILLE	3.11.16		to HYMMEVILLE and left our tilling billets there Ordinary Routine	
"	7.11.16		Escorted six sick horses by road to No 2 Veterinary Hospital ABBEVILLE	
"	9.11.16		" one " " " " " " " "	
"	13.11.16		" four " " " " " " " "	
"	15.11.16		" one " " " " " " " "	
"	18.11.16		" two " " " " " " " "	
"	20.11.16		" two " " " " " " " "	
"	21.11.16		" one " " " " " " " "	
"	26.11.16		Under orders received from Staff, split Unit into two Cavalry Brigades to work the M V S. marched to MOYENNVILLE and billeted there	
"	30.11.16		Escorted six sick horses by road to No 2 Veterinary Hospital ABBEVILLE	

B Saunders Capt.
for O.C.

[Stamp: MOBILE VETERINARY SECTION No. 1293 Date 30.11.16 LUCKNOW CAVALRY BDE]

SERIAL NO. 178.

Confidential

War Diary

of

Mobile Veterinary Section, Lucknow Cavalry Brigade.

FROM 1st December 1916 TO 31st December 1916.

No. 8

WAR DIARY.

OF

MOBILE VETERINARY SECTION.

For the month of

DECEMBER, 1916.

Army Form C. 2118.

WAR DIARY
or
INTELLIGENCE SUMMARY
(Erase heading not required.)

Instructions regarding War Diaries and Intelligence Summaries are contained in F. S. Regs, Part II. and the Staff Manual respectively. Title Pages will be prepared in manuscript.

Place	Date	Hour	Summary of Events and Information	Remarks and references to Appendices
MOYENNEVILLE	1.12.16		Ordinary Routine Work	
"	2.12.16		Evacuated three sick animals by road to No 2 V.H. Hospital ABBEVILLE	
"	5.12.16		" one " " " " " "	
"	8.12.16		" one " " " " " "	
"	9.12.16		" one " " Motor Ambulance to " "	
"	12.12.16		" one " " hospital to No 22 "	
"	14.12.16		The Mobile Veterinary Section marched to CHAUSSOY-LES-TEOUFLES and took over billets, equipment & detachment A.H.T. D.A.T. low D. from BOUILLANCOURT. Motor Ambulance 15 to 22 V.H. Hospital	
CHAUSSOY	17.12.16		" moved to No 22 V.H. Hospital	
"	19.12.16		" " " " " " "	
"	20.12.16		" " " M. Amb.	
"	"		" " " Bus. Stock	
"	"		" " " "	
"	27.12.16		" " " "	
"	28.12.16		" " " "	
"	31.12.16		D.D.V.S. Cavalry Corps inspected Section Ordinary Routine Work	

P. G. Carey Capt. a. V. C.
Comdg

[Stamp: MOBILE VETERINARY SECTION No. 2118 Date 31.12.16 LUCKNOW CAVALRY BDE.]

www.ingramcontent.com/pod-product-compliance
Lightning Source LLC
Chambersburg PA
CBHW081239170426
43191CB00034B/1985